How to Stop Being a Blind Witch *or Warlock*

by Dr. Marlene Miles
Freshwater Press 2024
freshwaterpress9@gmail.com

ISBN: 978-1-965772-54-6

Paperback Version

Table of Contents

How to STOP Being a
BLIND WITCH
or Warlock

Freshwater

Freshwater Press, USA

Lord, if I'm a blind witch, deliver me today, in the Name of Jesus. Amen.

I'm Not Calling You a Witch

I am not calling you a witch. Nor am I calling you a warlock if you are a male. However, it is not as though I have not noticed, found, run into, or been bumped into by witches or warlocks. With our spiritual eyes God shows us all kinds of things, does He not?

The Word of God says that witches will not inherit the kingdom, so we all should check ourselves to be sure that we are walking according to the Word if we want to make Heaven. Of all the things to play with, witchcraft is not one of those things.

Not only that, witches should not be living, according to the Word of God, so if those who practice witchcraft are slated for death and also for hell, we all need to get it right on *this* side before it's too late.

If you Google this, you will be misled and deceived. AI has decided that witches are okay but those who practice sorcery are malicious. There are many opinions about witchcraft in any online search or source, many of which probably written by witches. Another search result says that sorcerers are okay, but witches are bad. God is the correct source regarding this topic and God does not *do* witches. God does not abide witches, and sorcerers are in that ilk.

Even though witches have been categorized and ranked, there are no "good" witches. Just as the "little white lie" is still a lie with the same results and consequences as the bold face lie--, they are both still lies. A witch is a witch no matter how small or what kind. If you are saved, you must know this, If you are not saved, you can get saved, God hears repentance every day, even for witchcraft. Else, where would we all be?

> Thou shalt **not suffer a witch to live**. (Exodus 22:18)

I am not promoting homicide, murder, hurt or harm to any person; we do not war against flesh and blood. Our civil laws do not allow murder. Furthermore, in the Bible, accused witches were dealt with collectively by the town. But, as spiritually dull as the collective of people may be in any society, how will they even *discern* a witch or agree to collectively deal with that witch?

However, I am challenging you, Dear Reader, as I have challenged myself, that you do not allow a witch to live inside of **you**. Make sure you are not a witch. This book is about a personal account, not a witch hunt and there will be no trials as in medieval Europe or Salem, Massachusetts or in modern day Africa, India or other remote places.

As a Christian, **you** don't want to *accidentally* practice witchcraft of any kind. Anyone who chooses witchcraft –

I'm not talking to them. This book is for those who need to know more and to evaluate themselves with the help of the Holy Spirit to be sure they are **not** practicing witchcraft, especially if they want to make it to Heaven.

> You shall not eat anything with its blood. You shall not practice divination or soothsaying. (Leviticus 19:26)

Divination and soothsaying are both forms of witchcraft. Having a *familiar spirit* is how a lot of people "know things" is also witchcraft. Unsanctioned rebellion of any kind against authority is as the sin of witchcraft; sometimes God instructs people to rebel against oppression. But rebellion against God is assuredly a no-no.

> A man or a woman who has a ghost or a familiar spirit shall be put to death; they shall be pelted with stones—and the bloodguilt is theirs. (Leviticus 20:27)

Magic and the use of magic is witchcraft. The art of performing charms, spells, and rituals, to control people or events is witchcraft. You may find in your searches that some say magic is good, but Moses was opposing the "magic" of the magicians in Pharaoh's house because there was nothing good about it. Still, we think that it is wholesome because Walt Disney says it is. God says it is not; I'm with God on this.

Magic is evil since it is witchcraft or sorcery. Sorcery implies magic where powers are intentionally used for a harm. Witchcraft uses supernatural power through a pact with evil *spirits*; this power may be exerted involuntarily. Magic, witchcraft, and sorcery are thought of as under the control of the person using those modalities. I'll say this right now:

a. <u>Where</u> did the person get those powers?
b. <u>How</u> did the person get those powers?

Those two answers can tell you that neither magic, witchcraft, nor sorcery are of God. There's no way to paint them pretty. Furthermore:

c. It may start out a certain way, but that human, who is not in Christ, has far less power than the demon, devil, imp, or evil *spirit* that they are trying to use or control.

Usually not right away, but over time, they will be overpowered or overtaken, unless they call on Jesus. Will Jesus come to them? It depends on how deep they are into the occult and how long they've been in it. How sincere is their call? If they are even still alive and have not been turned over to a reprobate mind. Probably there are other parameters as well that the Lord knows as to whether He will come or not when they call.

Seek ye the Lord while he may be found, call ye upon him while he is near:

Let the wicked forsake his way, and the unrighteous man his thoughts: and let him return unto the Lord, and he will have mercy upon him; and to our God, for he will abundantly pardon. (Isaiah 55:6-7)

Humans need to stop playing with strange fire.

FYI: Occultism includes, angelology, alchemy, astrology, cartomancy (divination with playing cards or Tarot cards) channeling, divination, fortune-telling, Luciferianism, magic (also spelled, *magick*), numerology, Satanism, trance-channeling, Wicca, witchcraft and other practices.

- Witchcraft has it's own subsets of types:
- **Alexandrian Witch**
- **Arthurian Witch**
- **Astral Projection**
- **Baby Witch**
- **Black Magic**
- **Blind Witch**
- **Celtic Witch**
- **Ceremonial Witchcraft** Uses rituals and invocations to invoke *spirits*.
- **Cosmic Witch**
- **Coven Witch**
- **Crystal Witch**
- **Dianic Witchcraft**
- **Diviner**

- **Eclectic Witchcraft is** such as Shamanism, Reiki, Yoga, and Eastern philosophy.
- **Elemental Witchcraft uses e**arth, air, fire, water, and spirit
- **Egyptian Witchcraft is similar to** Wicca but invokes Egyptian deities.
- **Folk Witchcraft is** Folk magic passed down through a family.
- **Faery Witchcraft is** rooted in Irish and Scottish culture. Fairies, dwarves and elves are wicked, they belong to the dark side and are not things to play with.
- **Gardnerian Witchcraft** A secret, formal, version of Wicca.
- **Gray Witch**
- **Green Witchcraft**
- **Hearth Witchcraft** involves home magick herbalism, candles, and ritual cleaning.
- **Hedge Witch**
- **Hereditary witchcraft**
- **Kitchen Witchcraft -**magic is incorporated into cooking and baking.

Folks, I keep telling you, don't eat everywhere, don't eat everyone's cooking, and bless your food very well before you eat it.

- **Lunar Witch**
- **Red Witchcraft**
- **Sea Witch**
- **Solitary Witch**
- **White Magick**
- **Wicca - A** modern Pagan religion

This is a list of 30 or more different types of witches, although I saw a site that listed 45. I didn't want to click on that, sorry. But, I can sum this up with, if there is no such thing as witchcraft, why are there so many different kinds of something that doesn't exist? It is estimated that 60 to 80% of the world's population does not believe that witchcraft exists. I suppose that is why they teach their children to seek it out and park their children in front of movies and TV shows that are all about witchcraft. Then there are those who believe they can fight witchcraft with their powerful minds. *Really?*

Then there's another percentage of the population that are actually practicing witchcraft. *Do we even know?* Most practitioners of witchcraft are occultic and do not advertise. Do any of us even know unless the Holy Spirit reveals it to us? Do we know when witchcraft is being directed at us? What are the signs?

In other countries in Africa, India, Papua New Guinea there are still witch hunts and people are killed because of the accusations, especially if disease is involved or passed on to others. At the same time, in many African villages a "native doctor" or traditional healer is respected, yet they use witchcraft. These people are not Christians so we cannot ascribe Christian values to them.

Now the works of the flesh are manifest, which are these; Adultery, fornication, uncleanness, lasciviousness,

Idolatry, witchcraft, hatred, variance, emulations, wrath, strife, seditions, heresies,

Envyings, murders, drunkenness, revellings, and such like: of the which I tell you before, as I have also told you in time past, that they which do such things shall not inherit the kingdom of God.(Galatians 5:19-21)

Wishcraft

Wishcraft is a NOW Age (New Age) method for manifestation: a self-hypnosis used for manifestation.

FYI: Hypnosis is you vacating your body, rather like astral projecting. That is witchcraft.

Manifesting is witchcraft. Yes, manifesting, which includes visualization can be considered witchcraft, as some believe that it is combined with magic. Manifestation is the practice of directing "energy" to achieve specific outcomes, and some believe that pairing it with magic can give you more power to achieve your intentions. Who or what do you think those "energies" that you are directing actually are? They are evil *spirits*, masquerading as helpful spirits to do your bidding.

After that, you have made covenant with them and now you must do their bidding – for the rest of your life, unless by Jesus Christ you get out of it. If you do not get out of it, your children and your grandchildren may be blindsided. Unless they become saved and in Christ, they may find that they owe some spiritual entity for things that they did not buy. You actually made a purchase that neither you nor they could ever afford.

Faith is the evidence of things hoped for, therefore things that are hoped for can actually happen. Wishing can be more related to fantasy such as the person who wishes they were invisible for some reason or other (usually ungodly), or they wish they could fly. These are not congruent with gravity and other facts of reality. Yet, we wish people a Merry Christmas and we wish them a Happy New Year, as well we wish them happy birthdays, and then get them to make a wish--, so the use of it can be ambiguous.

Yet, with Faith we pray because we have hope. But different than "manifesting" we don't pray to ourselves, we don't pray to random or unknown spiritual energies, we pray to the Father, in the Name of Jesus.

Verily, verily, I say unto you, Whatsoever ye shall ask the Father in my name, he will give it you. Hitherto have ye asked nothing in my name: ask, and ye shall receive, that your joy may be full. (John 16:23-24)

We don't pray to known demonic entities because we are Christians. We especially don't because we do not mix religions. We do not mix the world with our own faith because that would be sacrilege.

That Woman Is a Witch

We have heard all too many men say that their ex is a witch. Certainly, we are tired of hearing that. But how many women don't **know** that or *if* they are witches? How many men don't even know that or if they are *warlocks*? Like attracts like. I know a fellow who seems to be attracted to witches, yet he is not Christian and has no real idea that they are witches.

Men, when you went home to meet the family, what did you look for? What did you see? Were you just seeing if the family was goodlooking and the mom aged well and kept her figure? Were you looking to see if they lived in a nice house and her daddy had money? What were you looking for? All natural, and nothing spiritual?

If a woman is not a witch until she stops doing what you want her to do, what does that make the man? The hallmarks of witchcraft are many. One is unforgiveness or anger or rage and desire for revenge. There is a desire for pay back. There is a desire for what one wants and only what one wants. There can be fury when a witch is not getting their way.

So, it stands that when a relationship breaks up, the dumper or the *dump-ee* are both angry that the other person is no longer doing their bidding. This is how witches behave, so how can one call the other a witch?

Well, this is where witches come from:

Your mother was or is a witch: then you're a witch or a warlock, depending on your gender. It's automatic.

How so?

It's in your blood. There are markers in your blood that scream witchcraft. Those markers are invisible, but they are picked up in the spirit.

It's amazing how many evil things we inherit, but we have to pursue the good things. Evil *spirits* come along with the flesh and the territory, but the good ones, such as the Holy Spirit, we have to ask for. We have to receive salvation and then ask for the Holy Spirit, even tarry for it, as the old folks used to say.

Your father was or is a warlock; you're a witch or a warlock, depending on your gender.

You were born into it. It is in your bloodline, somewhere, then it's in you.

A woman was so proud of her families "special gifts" to see things and know things. If this is not of God via giftings of the Holy Spirit, then it is done by a *familiar spirit.* Most of what is known by a *familiar spirit* is from the past. *Why*? Because this *spirit* has been living with and observing, and also influencing your family for thousands of years. It knows all your family business and history. So, by the time you decide to do something stupid like have a séance you will get a *familiar spirit* that is familiar with your family and able to impersonate almost any dead person in your bloodline. In so doing they can tell you all kinds of stuff, some may be true, but most won't be. Don't do this.

Evil dedication- A parent, sibling, or any other blood relative can dedicate you for evil. That is like nominating you for the dark kingdom. The devil decides to do with you as he chooses. Marry you? it's a possibility. Use you, based on your gifts and God-given virtues? Possibly. Sacrifice you? Also, a possibility. Any and all of these things could happen, and you may know nothing about it. It could happen as soon as birth or even before. Unless you get saved and know Christ and get delivered, you are in the clutches of evil. These nominated or initiated people have unfortunate lives and wonder why life doesn't go well for them. Yes, any blood relative can do this to you. This is why the work of a parent is seriously full time, protecting their child physically, emotionally, and especially spiritually. Even from relatives.

Evil initiation is when you have been initiated into witchcraft whether you know it or not.

You see yourself flying in the dream. You're a witch. You don't have to be on a broom, you could just be flying. You may not be on a magic carpet or in a plane, but you are flying, either solo or with someone. You're a witch. If you didn't sign up to be a witch, then you've either been dedicated or initiated. Initiation can be in ignorance, willingly, or unwillingly, with your knowledge or without it.

You dream, even once, of being in coven meetings; you're a witch. Especially if you have dreamed this more than once, you are a witch. Why would witches want you there? If you are weak spiritually, they can use you in any number of ways and you won't even know you got used.

You hate your co-worker, what a coincidence, so do the witches, or they need a sacrifice, or they want to steal from your co-worker. Well, you're at work with this person 5 days a week so the witches can use you as a *monitoring spirit*, a spy to let them know what's going on with your co-worker. You get summoned into a coven meeting at night while you are asleep and you talk, talk, talk, and spill tea to the coven.

This could even happen if you love your co-worker, but you are spiritually weak.

You wake up the next morning, but the "dream" has been wiped, you have no idea that you've done this. You have no idea that you work for witches. When you are in alliance with some folks, you are one of them. You are a devil agent. Folks, this is why we pray for deliverance from things that we know not of. This is why we pray for Mercy every time we pray dangerous and judgmental prayers unless we absolutely, positively know that we are not working for Satan, unawares.

You use control, manipulation, domination or intimidation on others to get your way; then you are a witch.

You believe in **magic**. You are interested in magic.

You are extremely interested in **witchy things, dark things, occultic things**, **satanic** things, and you may not even realize it.

Halloween is your favorite "holiday." Oh, don't get me started on how people worship Halloween. There is a house in my neighborhood that is so done up for Halloween that I have to turn my head and pray when I drive past it. Somehow, mysteriously on November 1st, it is as done up for Christmas as it was for Halloween. And I mean the next day, folks. What God are they serving? Do they even know?

You love spooky, scary, horror, and dark genres of movies, books, stories, and TV shows.

You have a familiar spirit that you spend time with and get information from but you may call it a spirit guide or a guardian spirit. *It's a demon.*

Ouija Board, works by *familiar spirits* and can invite a lot of other demons.

You are **superstitious**. You believe old wives' tales.

You seek out and believe **horoscopes**. **Astrology** and horoscope info comes from the second heaven, where the seat of Satan is. So, you wake up in the morning and check your horoscope which is the same as deciding that you will ask Satan how your day will be. Horoscopes are vague, general, or part truth and mostly lies. If you believe in it, you will make it happen by self-fulfilling the evil prophecy. You can take it and make it fit into your day and your life and after doing this for a while you can be stuck in it. Nancy Regan brough astrologers to the White House, you can imagine what that released over the country.

Horoscopes include zodiac signs. Folks, every zodiac "sign" has an accompanying idol *god.* When you claim that sign, that idol claims you. Many of these and other idol *gods* and *goddesses* are hidden in college frats and sorority pledges.

Games of chance, raffles, and lotteries are lorded over by Asmodeus who is also a *god* of divorce. Wages, betting, and gambling are things the world uses as entertainment. They are ungodly and witchy things to do.

Other witchy things include:

Astral projection

Automatic writing

ESP

Clairvoyance

Clairaudience

Fortune telling of any kind, from crystal balls to Tarot card readings--, either giving or receiving them

You believe in **luck.**

Lucky charms (not the breakfast cereal) but now that I mention it, do you see how idols get their worship? Teach a kid to like this 'magically delicious' cereal and they will be calling the name over and again through their childhood. What is this doing? Invoking devils, imps, demons and evil *spirits*. It doesn't happen on the same day, it takes a while, but before you know it here comes something that no one expected into the life of your child, your family, your house. What would have inspired the cereal maker to name a cereal this, anyway?

If you do **rituals**, then you are likely a witch.

Marrying a witch or warlock, or even having sex with a witch or warlock initiates you. When you have **sex** with a person you become what that person is. You become one flesh with that person.

That is why and how marriages are consummated. When you mate with a person one of you may get consumed--, or both of you. Men who love to accuse women of being witches--, then why are you dating witches? Why would you marry one?

You need to keep your eyes open, because witches may show up for a date in a little black dress, but the black, pointy hat is usually left at home. Same goes for men, I've never met one who wore a long black cape on a date, although he may have wanted to wave his 'magic wand' after the dinner was over. That date could be a whole warlock, yet he may or may not know that he is.

Folks, we have to ask God who these people are that we meet in life and date or want to date. *God, who is his person to you?* I asked that just last night and the response I got in my dream was hilarious, but true. I cannot repeat it, however. If God answered me, then He will also answer you. Instead of just your friends, ask God about the person you are interested in.

Going to certain **festivals** and music concerts can initiate you into witchcraft and the occult. Whatever *god* they are serving, you will be serving.

Making covenant or alliances in any other way with a witch or warlock, as in friendships, situationships, marriages can initiate you into witchcraft.

Money seals covenants; did you receive money or other gifts? Did you give them?

Food can seal a covenant; did you eat food that the other person made and or paid for?

Evil handshake can initiate a person.

Evil laying on of hands can initiate one into the dark kingdom, as a witch or warlock. Evil prophecy by false prophets and false pastors. People of God, the fake or false prophet or pastor has to recruit people for darkness; this is a pyramid scheme. In order for them to get to the top, stay on top, or not be killed, themselves, they need folks below them. Don't let it be you.

An **evil name** can initiate a person. Whatever you are called, especially if it is the name of an idol, can initiate a person.

Sacrificing to idols does not just include food. A person can offer a sacrifice to an idol and not even realize they did it. Ever throw money in a wishing well? What was down there? Who did you throw the money to?

Evil garments such as Halloween costumes. Evil garments such as those worn in the **white garment "church"** can initiate.

Jack-O-Lantern at your front door dedicates your youngest child; it tells the devil that he can have your youngest.

I'm not saying you can never go anywhere or have any fun. Check with the Holy Spirit, He will lead you into all Truth. It depends on how deep you are into anything dark and evil as to what you can and can't do to get out and stay out. It depends on the foundation of your bloodline as well as any dedications and your own sins and initiations.

Revoke evil parental dedication or dedication by unknown others. Be sure you are saved and dedicated to God. God cannot bless you if you have been pre-dedicated to evil *spirits*, family idols, or other evil entities, until you break the first dedication.

And they shall put my name upon the children of Israel; and I will bless them. (Numbers 6:27)

1. Lord, have Mercy on me, a sinner. I confess my sins, the sins of my parents, and the sins of my ancestors, going all the way back to Adam & Eve. Lord, forgive us, in the Name of Jesus.
2. Lord, remove all iniquity from my bloodline, in the Name of Jesus.
3. Blood of Jesus, separate me from the sins of my ancestors, in the Name of Jesus.

4. I renounce every evil dedication placed upon my life, in the Name of Jesus.
5. I renounce and loose myself from every evil dedication, in the Name of Jesus.
6. Lord, if I am a blind witch, deliver me today, in the Name of Jesus.
7. Every demon associated with the evil dedication, leave me now, I divorce you now, in the Name of Jesus.
8. I break every evil curse up against me, I am in Christ, I am in Jacob and no enchantment can stand against Jacob, in the Name of Jesus.
9. Father, cancel all evil consequences of broken demonic promise or dedication, in the Name of Jesus.
10. Broken dedication, you will not backfire on me, in the Name of Jesus.
11. Demons of the dedication, you are bound from retaliating against me, or regrouping against me by the Power in the Blood of Jesus.
12. All demons, devils, evil *spirits*, and entities associated with this now

broken dedication depart from me now and forever, in the Name of Jesus.

13. By the power in the Blood of Jesus I destroy every evil dedication made by my parents, even if they meant well, in the Name of Jesus.
14. I renounce every evil dedication
15. Every evil ancestral name, I renounce and reject it. I break the power of every evil dedication ever placed on my head in the Name of Jesus.
16. I break every evil pledge, vow, promise, or covenant ever made on my behalf, in the Name of Jesus.

Being dedicated to evil is under the Curse of the Law.

Christ hath redeemed us from the curse of the law, being made a curse for us: for it is written, Cursed is every one that hangeth on a tree:

That the blessing of Abraham might come on the Gentiles through Jesus Christ; that we might receive the promise of the Spirit through faith.
(Galatians 3:13-14)

Amen.

Witchcraft *Adjacent*

You'd be surprised at how many things are witchcraft or witchcraft *adjacent,* and right next to a very slippery slope. These things seem innocent, but they are either witchcraft or so close that they are spiritually hazardous. This world is full of evil potholes, witchcraft chief among them.

Using crystals for protection, or whatever they are for is witchy. Crystals are used for spells, stones are used for spells and sometimes crystals are used for healing. Folks, the devil doesn't heal; he comes not but for to steal, kill, and destroy. If it looks like the devil is healing, all he is doing is commanding the disease to lie dormant for a while so the person thinks they are healed. Or, he may jump the disease over to another person. He is in no way getting rid of the disease. The devil doesn't heal. He comes to steal, kill, and destroy. All the other stuff that anyone is calling on him to do is not really going to happen. It may *appear* as if it is happening, but it is not.

The blessings of the Lord maketh rich and he adds no sorrow with it. (Proverbs 10:22)

If you have an aversion to God, Jesus, the Church, or things related to Christianity, this is an *anti-Christ spirit*. You are not interested in church or anything related to God, this is witchy, and it is anti-Christ.

Seeing Jesus signs and Bibles does something to you. I met a woman once who said that her neighbor's signage makes her crazy. I had a man to yell at me, very loudly for believing in God. We were supposed to have been friends.

That at the name of Jesus every knee should bow, of things in heaven, and things in earth, and things under the earth;

And that every tongue should confess that Jesus Christ is Lord, to the glory of God the Father. (Philippians 2:10-11)

The demons in these people do not want to bow but they know they must. All that yelling, screaming and protesting is their demons manifesting at the appearance of Jesus or anything related to Him or His Spirit. At the mention of His Name, even reading His Name. Think of Legion, what did he say? *Why have you come here to torment us?* These people are under torment by the Name of Jesus. All the more shouldn't they be by your presence if you carry the Spirit of God within you?

You can't choose your family but choose your "friends" wisely; some of them may be into witchcraft or witchcraft *adjacent*. It doesn't mean they are practicing it on you, it means that the spirit of witchcraft is with them and their walk and talk will show it. A witchy friend is the type to tell you to withhold sex from your spouse until that spouse gives you what you want. That is witchcraft.

How Could This Have Happened?

It could have happened to any one by a witchcraft initiation dream. *Flying--*, if you are flying in a dream, you have been initiated into witchcraft. Especially if you see yourself:

- Landing in a place surrounded by strangers.
- Landing in a place of satanic people.
- In a place of altars.
- In a strange place with strange people.

Then pray very seriously because initiation into the kingdom of darkness can happen if you have not declared who you are for. If your spirit man is weak and unfed and you are dry and prayerless, you could be overtaken by evil. If you have certain spiritual gifts that the dark kingdom thinks it could use, they will initiate you into darkness. You may not know a thing about it. If you came from a background of witchcraft and you have markers in your blood, they see you as one of *theirs*. Again, you may not know a thing about it.

Watch out for all of this, although this may not be all that there is. Evil initiation can happen in the dream by the following.

- Food—eating in the dream.
- Drinking in the dream.
- FLYING.
- Flying into water.
- Flying into forests.
- Seeing witches, as in a coven.
- Seeing yourself in a club and whatever is happening is spiritual, but it is not a church, and it is not Godly, and you are being forced to do what they are doing.
- Partying with famous people –this is a witchcraft initiation.
- Sex in the dream.

Remember, a famous or celebrity face could be the face of a masquerade. Therefore, I'm not saying that famous people are witches, but I'm not saying that they aren't either. Many wear their witchcraft as a badge of honor; they are proud of it.

17. Any power that has been initiating me in the night, let me go, in the Name of Jesus.

18. I refuse to be a part of witchcraft covenants, and covens, in the Name of Jesus.
19. Any initiation on my life, I break it, in the Name of Jesus. (Fast and pray.)
20. Lord, show me the secret behind my problem, in the Name of Jesus.
21. LORD, show me the secrets to my long-standing problems, in the Name of Jesus.

Pray very well over all the food you eat in the natural. Sanctify it, in the Name of Jesus.

Prayers Against Evil Initiation

22. Blood of Jesus, cover me.
23. Lord, I bless You, for You alone are holy. Bless Your Holy Name. Thank You for your great love and mercy towards me, in the Name of Jesus.
24. Thank You Father that I can come boldly to Your Throne of Grace to obtain Grace and Mercy in this time of great need, in the Name of Jesus.
25. Even though I am afflicted, Thank You, Lord that You have not turned me over to death, in the Name of Jesus.
26. Lord, You are mighty; You are a warrior, the Lord is Your Name. To You be all the praise.
27. Father, I have made some missteps, please forgive me and bring me back from the dark side or the brink of the Darkside, in the Name of Jesus.
28. By the power in the Blood of Jesus, I renounce every evil agreement,

covenant, contract and initiation into witchcraft, in the Name of Jesus.

29. Thank You Lord, for Salvation in Christ Jesus.

30. Thank You Lord, for restoring right position in the spirit, in the Name of Jesus.

31. Thank You, Lord for the authority to pray these prayers, in the Name of Jesus Christ.

32. Father, I ask for Your Mercy in every way I have opened my life up to attacks from the enemy, „let Your Mercy speak for me, in the mighty Name of Jesus.

33. Lord, please forgive me for not obeying Your Word and not living by your precepts. Let Your Mercy speak for me, in the Name of Jesus.

34. Please forgive me, Father for all the times I've associated with the wrong people, let Your Mercy prevail over my case, Lord, in the Name of Jesus.

35. Lord, forgive me if I've been the wrong person who has led others astray, in the Name of Jesus.

36. Lord, arise and fight for me against those that are contending with me, in the Name of Jesus.
37. I reject every evil initiation, in the mighty Name of Jesus Christ.
38. Whenever my name is mentioned for evil, Holy Ghost Fire, answer for me, in the mighty Name of Jesus Christ
39. Every gathering of witches where I am summoned, LORD I won't go. Holy Spirit put a wall of Fire between me and them and keep me out of their presence and their meetings, in the Name of Jesus.
40. Evil gathering of witches and councils against my destiny, scatter now by Fire, in the mighty Name of Jesus Christ.
41. I command every evil decree and ordinance written against me and my family to be wiped off now by the Blood of Jesus Christ.
42. Lord, silence every evil human agent working against me by witchcraft or occultism, in the Name of Jesus.
43. I reject every evil gift meant to initiate me into an occultic or satanic cult or

witchcraft coven, in the mighty Name of Jesus Christ.

44. I decree that I am seated in heavenly places far above principalities and powers, therefore the devil shall not gain access into my life, in the Name of Jesus.

45. I decree that no weapon formed against me and my family shall prosper, in the Name of Jesus Christ.

46. Demonic aggression against me from the pit of hell, go back and destroy your senders, in the Name of Jesus.

47. I belong to Christ; I am in Christ, therefore devil and all your agents, get out of my life by the power in the Blood of Jesus.

48. I shall live and I shall not die, my family and I shall live to tell of the goodness of God in the land of the living, in the Name of Jesus Christ.

49. There shall be no sudden disaster in my family, in the Name of Jesus.

50. Every incantation, enchantment and divination made against me and my family, I command it to go back and

destroy the senders; I demand it, in the Name of Jesus Christ.

51. In this season, I shall suffer no loss, in the Name of Jesus.

52. Lord, let every plan of the wicked that is against me and destiny, fall to the ground, in the Name of Jesus.

53. I render all evil covenants made against my life useless by the power in the Blood of Jesus.

54. Lord, free me from the powers of darkness and their evil works, in the mighty Name of Jesus Christ

55. I am in Christ; I serve Him only, in the Name of Jesus.

56. I refuse to belong to any evil group, society, or council, in the Name of Jesus Christ.

57. The devil shall not have a foothold in my life, in the Name of Jesus Christ.

58. I will make a joyful noise unto the Lord, and I will come before His presence with singing, for all the marvelous things He has done for me. Amen.

59. Thank You, Father for answering my prayers, in Jesus' Name. Amen.

That Mouth

That mouth gossips among other grievous, witchy things.

Out of the same mouth proceed blessing and cursing. (James 3:10)

We need to watch the way we talk. Say only what helps because each word is a gift, (MSG Bible).

Curse words are different than cursing a person, although curse words can be used when cursing a person.

Let no corrupt communication proceed out of your mouth, but that which is good to the use of edifying, that it may minister grace unto the hearers.

And grieve not the holy Spirit of God, whereby ye are sealed unto the day of redemption.

Let all bitterness, and wrath, and anger, and clamour, and evil speaking, be put away from you, with all malice:

And be ye kind one to another, tenderhearted, forgiving one another, even as God for Christ's sake hath forgiven you. (Ephesians 4:29-32)

Oh the things that come out of our mouths--, all of us need to choose what we say wisely.

We all speak and the person who is a blind witch, does not even realize that they are speaking curses, and they are cursing people. They speak most of the time out of their flesh. They speak out of anger, jealousy, fear, unforgiveness, and the desire for revenge, hatred, discord, rage, rivalries, divisions, factions, envy, drunkenness and the like.

In a nice way, in the world, we call them *petty*. Being called petty is so much more than just petty, it is tacky and revengeful, it is tit for tat, it is a *payback spirit* as it is used in today's vernacular. People adopt the term for themselves and wear it boldly. One woman told me she was petty and proud of it. Petty does not mean trivial or less than as it says in the dictionary, it means spiteful. It is driven by pride.

And I warn you more than those who do such things will not inherit the Kingdom of God. (Galatians 5:21)

So, when you start the evil talk, when you start discord and gossip and rumors, that's blind witchcraft.

Be ye angry, and sin not: let not the sun go down upon your wrath: neither give place to the devil. (Ephesians 4:26)

When anger starts to speak, anger says things like, *You know, you're getting on my last nerve, I'm gonna do A, B, and C to you.* With that kind of threat, you may just send a person into survival mode. You may have really scared them and brought them anxiety. They may become seriously agitated and this may diminish the person's ability to perform and succeed, either that day, at that moment, later in life, or ever in life.

Your words or the words of the person who spoke in anger and harshly to another person is a form of blind witchcraft. When hatred speaks, it's probably just the same as anger speaking. When jealousy speaks, saying something like, *Aww man, I don't know what you think you did but it can do that.* So instead of celebrating a successful person, even a successful child or successful friend, and encouraging them to reach higher, the blind witch cuts them down.

When covetousness speaks it sounds like, *I wish I had that. I wish I had your ____. I wish my child was better than yours.* Covetousness is New Testament idolatry. Idolatry is a work of the flesh, listed just before witchcraft in Galatians.

Sometimes parents are jealous of their own children, and I've also seen children who are jealous of their parents. There is deliverance for all of this.

A child, for instance, may not know if a parent is jealous of them for years, or even forever since it is so unexpected. A child expects love from their parents and jealousy is diametrically opposed to *agape* love. So, the words that a parent speaks carry all authority and can be deeply positive or deeply negative to the child.

We are talking about witchcraft, so it is to the negative even if the speaker is a *blind witch*.

When fear speaks, for instance, a parent may say to a child, *"Don't you go out on those streets, X,Y,Z is going to happen to you if you go out there."* And, before you know it X,Y, and Z happens to that child. This is self-fulfilling prophecy and it was an evil prophecy. Prophets of God do not speak evil, defeatist, lying words; they speak the Word of God.

Blind witches on the other hand - that mouth of theirs could be issuing curses like bullets and they don't even realize how powerful their mouths are.

It would have been better to speak protection over that child. It would have been better to speak wisdom and instill in them the desire to either be home or somewhere productive, doing something worthwhile. That would have been better than reporting to the child what's in the street, and expressing your fear over what may happen to your child, because your fear is what you call, love.

60. Lord, do not let me be a blind witch, even in the name of Love, in the Name of Jesus. Amen.

These are voices of the flesh, things people speak when they are in their flesh. And there are many more *voices*. Know this: Flesh tends to witchcraft. You see a witch? They are not walking by the Spirit, they are in their flesh doing what they want, when they want, their way. The Word says we shall know them by their fruit. Witches have no Fruit of the Spirit because they are not connected to the Holy Spirit; but they can act. They can pretend to be the nicest, sweetest, softest-spoken people in the world. Oh please. So discern.

They are tending to their *I-wants.* It's fear, it's worry, it's anxiety. It tends to witchcraft, even *blind witchcraft.*

When the person doesn't even realize that their **words** are so destructive. Whether you use cuss words or swear words or not, this is speaking curses over people. Speaking curses blindly is blind witchcraft, and this person is called a blind witch.

When drunkenness is allowed to speak--, do we have any idea what a drunk person is going to say? Yeah, if we know that drunk. But there are nice drunks, evil drunks, quiet drunks, loud and belligerent drunks. Either way, their words are not to be trusted. A mean drunk can spew out virulent and damaging words, and their words should not be internalized.

When frustration talks, *"Good grief. Can't you do anything right? Can't you even find your own shoes? You'd lose your head if it wasn't attached to your neck. I'm so tired of having to pick up after you. Are you helpless?*

That's frustration talking, speaking a curse. As said, you don't have to use curse words or profanity to curse. You're telling a person what's wrong with them all the time. God doesn't do that to us. The words of the faithless, words are flung at a person. Sometimes the person may not ever hear these words, but they're out there.

One faithless parent may in private say this to the other parent, *"You know, I don't think Junior is good at baseball."*

The other parent may escalate, *"You know that boy can't do anything right."* Dad, did you just curse your boy's life, his hands, his livelihood, his purpose because he can't play baseball? Are you serious right now?

Dad is an avid sports fan. Maybe he's a veteran athlete from his own time in high school or college, and he wants his boy to be a baseball player too. But he sums it all up with, *"No, that boy's not going to amount to anything."*

These are all word curses. Maybe Junior is not supposed to be a baseball player. Maybe he's supposed to be something else. We are to learn who our children are, and train them up in the way they should go, not train them up in the way we want them to go. These are all word curses spoken by the blind witchcraft of a witch or a warlock.

Junior may not have even heard any of these words in the natural, but the words are *out there* now and spoken by an authority over the kid. They're word curses. So even if a person is not good at a task that doesn't mean they're not good at something else, perhaps they are just in the wrong position.

It would be better to encourage your child, and if they fail, they fail rather than to have your words push them or drive them into failure. O, ye of little faith.

Childish Children & Desperate Adults

Understandably, childish vows, oaths and childish declarations can be made such as, *"When I grow up, I'm never--. And I'm never gonna do this, I'm never gonna do that or the other."*

Or, *"You know what? I'm <u>always</u> gonna do this and this, that, and the other."* Also, blind witchcraft, I suppose by a *baby blind witch*. Parents, you must listen to what your children say and always teach and correct them.

Then we have desperate adults who behave as adolescents. They say things such as, *"The next man that comes through that door."* I saw this in a movie plot, and you probably have too. These are desperate wannabe housewives. The women who hunt men and they want desperately to be married, so they might say, *The next man that comes through that door* --, and some of them mean it and that is *blind witchcraft.*

I feel sorry for the man.

It's a common movie plot; men do it too. They may say, *The next woman that comes through those doors.* These men are planning their own strategies for or against whoever is coming through that door.

It's all chance, the casting of lots as it were. In the Old Testament, lots were cast. But now we have the Holy Spirit. You can just pray and listen for the answers to your prayers. You don't have to leave things to chance. No need to put out a fleece as in Judges 6:40.

And Jephthah vowed a vow unto
the Lord, and said, If thou shalt without
fail deliver the children of Ammon into
mine hands, Then it shall be, that

whatsoever cometh forth of the doors of my house to meet me, when I return in peace from the children of Ammon, shall surely be the Lord's, and I will offer it up for a burnt offering.

So Japheth crossed over to the Ammonites to fight against him, and the Lord delivered them into his hand. (Judges 11:30-31)

The rest of that story is that the first thing that came out of his house was his child.

It is not wise to make soulish vows and prayers. It is not wise because the devil gets into every kind of soulish talk, every kind of soulish prayer, every soulish vow, soulish oath, and soulish covenant. The devil gets in it, and he will change it to *wish*craft, devil craft, or whatever kind of craft he can turn it in to. The devil will hurt the person that spoke to as well as the person to whom it is directed. He doesn't care what you **meant** to say. He doesn't care what you really wanted. The devil gets in where he can fit in.

Reverse Psychology

To me, reverse psychology and attempts at reverse psychology are the worst. Reverse psychology is a method where you try to get someone to do something you want them to do by challenging them that they *can't* do it. Or, by pretending you don't want them to do what you really want them to do.

Please show me where God **ever** did this. To me, this is lying, and we know that God cannot lie. The Scriptures say let your yes be yes, and let your no be no because anything else comes from the evil one.

To me, reverse psychology and would-be reverse psychology are the worst. And, because some people aren't even good at it, they are just speaking their passive-aggressive words. Depending on the person's position over the person that they're speaking to and how many times they hear it, as well as the temperament of the person who receives these words, it could be really debilitating to their life. It could oppress them entirely, for life.

This person—the hearer of this fake psychology, may not even do what you **want** them to do--, they may end up doing the thing you **spoke** and not the *opposite* of the thing you spoke.

They may not be strong enough to overcome the authority that you hold over them. Remember, faith comes by hearing.

Selfish words also curse, blindly. For instance, a parent secretly or doesn't want their child to leave home, they want their child to stay home--, it doesn't matter which child. Let's say he's the oldest child--, the only male. Or, he's the favorite, the favorite son. Or it could be that he's the youngest one. No matter which one it is, the parent wants this child to stay at home with them forever. You know, as the parent ages, as they get older or maybe they need support, such as financial, medical, health-related support. So, the parent begins to speak that word curse over the child – you know, soulish talk.

You're going to stay right here with me, aren't you?

I've heard loving children, four and five years old saying to the parent, *"When I grow up, I'm never leaving you."* And the parent never corrects them; the parent may encourage it. Perhaps this is a very needy parent. Perhaps it's an egotistical parent who wants to be the favorite parent. Whatever the reason, this may be why you see people that are 40 or 50 years old--, mostly men, who've never left home because of those words, those word curses spoken by *blind witches*.

False obligations, false loads, evil loads put on people. Especially if there is a loss in the family, if the husband is lost early due to death, or if there's a divorce. You can't tell a seven-year-old that he's now the man of the house. He's seven! You may have just sucked up that child's whole life, and put an evil load on him.

No, it's not the husband's fault because he left, well---, unless the father of the boy told him something stupid like that. That boy is not his mother's husband and he's not a man; he's seven. He has no authority in that house over his mother; he is a child. When he gets his own house, he can be an authority. Or maybe Dad wants him to come over to his house and run it. He's seven.

And that's hardly much different than if a child is lost, or if a child goes off to college, you can't just go down the block, down the street and get another kid and say, *"OK, come over to my house, you're my kid now."* You can't do it unless you're in a really bad movie. And if your children are grown, thank God. If they've left home and they're doing their thing, and functioning, thank God.

You want company, companionship? Get some new activities, get some new hobbies, get a dog, get some new friends, Grow in life. Grow spiritually; grow in God.

Do not try to control your life to stay the same. That is witchcraft, control, domination, manipulation, intimidation. It is all witchcraft. It is all *blind witchcraft* if you don't realize that you're doing it.

Devil Proof Your Words

You need to consider your words-, you, me--, all of us. We need to consider our words. Would God ever say anything like this? The words you're speaking, would you want anyone to speak words like this over you?

Devil proof your words. Consider how and if the devil can use any words or phrases or sentences that you are speaking **against** you, or anyone else. Be really clear in your statements. Finish every thought and every word that you speak.

Don't let the devil use your own words against you. Have you heard people say that they're just sick and tired of ____?

(You can fill in the blanks.) They're sick and tired of ____ .

Don't say that.

Personally, I'm **not** sick and I'm **not** tired. Even if I am, I won't speak it out like that. Saints of God, if you walk in authority, in God, if you walk in authority in the Spirit, you should never throw words out like ping pong balls, Not any word, not any phrase. If I were to experience any symptom of sick or tired, or sick *and* tired, I would tell it to God, I would pray and I would say, "By Jesus' stripes, I am healed." (Isaiah 53:5) then, I'd be believing for healing and deliverance.

If I were tired, I would say. But they that wait upon the Lord shall renew their strength, they shall run and not be weary. They shall walk and not faint (Isaiah 40:31)

Of course, if you went to medical personnel, you would have to report your symptoms. That's another whole thing, and I'm not talking about that. I'm talking about randomly proclaiming these words without devil proofing them may give the devil the open door to bring sick and or tired upon you. Don't use blind witchcraft on yourself. Careful of the words you speak.

Careful of slang, jargon, and street lingo. The phrase that somebody is killing it, or killing something? Whatever *it* is. I don't even know what *it* is. No, I don't use phrases like that.

NO, I'm not saying that I'm better than anybody who is reading this. I'm simply telling you about myself, because nothing is killing me or anyone or anything that I know.

Thank you Lord, I don't speak or own phrases like that. Did you know that very phrase was popular back in 1970s? I know of a guy who used to say stuff like that all the time and his life has ended up being strangely negative.

Proclaiming curses over yourself--, being a blind witch. Not even realizing that you are hurting yourself when you're using these negative words. Don't speak death over yourself. Speak life over yourself and over your life's situations.

Now if I'm in the spirit and we are in warfare, that's a whole different thing. If we're *killing* the work and or the enemies of God in the spirit, that's another whole thing entirely in spiritual warfare. Amen.

Hyperbole can be blind witchcraft. Exaggerated statements are hyperbole which are words and claims that aren't meant to be taken literally. You may see why or how things are taken literally when you didn't mean them literally

Here's an example of hyperbole. *"Do I have to say this a million times before you understand?* Well, you just told that person that they are dumb. If you are set in authority over that person and they believe you, you just took their self-esteem down a notch or two.

Yeah. Remember, faith comes by hearing (Romans 10:17).

What you just said to them may have been the last time that they needed to hear something like that to make their confidence plummet. And then they may, for the rest of their lives fulfill the prophecy that you spoke over them, over time--, by giving up. This could have even been your spouse, or your kid.

Blind witch, you didn't mean to do that, did you? You didn't mean to destroy a person, did you?

I've never meant to hurt people with my words, just the enemies of God, not humans, not people.

Self-Talk

So, we're back in Ephesians 4, and I ask you, did your words administer Grace to the hearer?

Do your words build a person up? Then perhaps it was a word curse that you spoke--, blindly. Blind witchcraft.

How about this one? This one you fill in the blank. This ____ will be the death of ___. Don't say that. It may seem clever and kind of cute, but you are in the Kingdom of God. You sit in authority. Your words carry weight.

Let no corrupt communication flow out of your mouth. Let no corrupt communication proceed out of your mouth, but that which is good to the use of edifying, that it may administer grace to the hearer.

Who would corrupt communication?

The prince of the power of the air. The one who sponsors confusion and misunderstandings, and fights, and divisions, *corruption* and wars. The one who wants to get into your words, because you, in Christ, have a superior authority than he does, and he wants to either usurp it or thwart it.

Don't let him; don't let your words be corrupted. It could make you into a blind witch.

Saints of God, sometimes you're the only hearer. Maybe you're at home or at work and you are just muttering or talking to yourself. Careful what your frustrations speak. Don't say bad things about yourself to yourself. Don't say bad things about yourself out loud. As a matter of fact, use your own words to encourage yourself. Encourage others. But David encouraged himself in the Lord.

- *You can do it.*
- *You can make it.*
- *You will succeed, in Jesus' Name.*

And David was greatly distressed because the people spake of stoning him because of the soul of all the people were grieved. Every man for his sons and his daughters, but David encouraged himself in the Lord his God.
(1Samuel 30:6)

Your self-talk says a lot about who you are. Your self-talk can lead to your success or failure. You need to be speaking self-affirmations, but don't leave God out of your affirmations, or they become as idolatry and self-worship. Do not speak self-condemnation.

While you're at it, speak affirmatively over others rather than condemning them.

There's no condemnation in Christ Jesus,
(Romans 8:1)

Words Have a Future

Consider the future of your words. God says, **The words that I speak they are Spirit, and they are life**.

Aren't we created in God's image and likeness? Then our words also have power. Maybe we wish some of the words that we have written or spoken had not been given life, or breath. Some may wish that those words could be forgotten, ot that certain words spoken would die. Consider that the words you speak, they are spirit, and they are life, as well, they live on into the future.

The words that God speaks are faithful; His words are more powerful than just regular words. The Word of God performs. His Words will not return to Him void. They will accomplish what God sends them to do, (Isaiah 55:11)

Don't you want to be that kind of person, like God? A person who's respected as what you say is real? Is it true, it's good, and it comes to pass?

You don't want to just say clown words, do you? Don't speak words that don't make any sense, words with no power. Because we're going to give an account of every word spoken.

Remember, your words are taken literally as they put angels to flight. Angels are sent to make what you just said happen for you. If they're good words, then the angels of God are going to try to make what you just said happened *for* you. If they are ignorant or evil words, then the devil's fallen angels will try to make what you just said happen **to** you. Or if you spoke that evil over another person to try to make what you just said happen *to* them.

Unless you spoke those words over or to a saint of God, then all of those words may be coming back against you. Because that other saint of God knows how to pray, and they know how to return evil words back to sender.

God has Angels to work on your behalf, and the devil has fallen angels to work against you. As far as I know, there are no clown angels who just laugh and do nothing when a person speaks unless you have no credibility, and no authority in the spirit. You are not a joke, so don't be a joker. I don't want to be a laughingstock; I want to be a person who can decree and declare a thing in authority when I need to handle spiritual business in the Earth.

Since you're saved and set in authority and seated at the right hand of the Father in Christ Jesus, that's royalty. Royalty lives in palaces, and in a palace, a laughing clown might be called a court jester. In the book of Revelation, a very serious Book, there is no description of such a thing. So there's no reason for us to play with words and to just throw them out there like confetti.

Heaven doesn't have court jesters. But when you're thinking about what to say to a person, over a person, or about a person, let Wisdom have its perfect work. Let Wisdom be at work here. Before you speak or proclaim something such as, "That woman can't cook, she'll never get a husband," stop and think first.

We don't know that. Well, we may know that she can't cook, but that doesn't mean our future statements about her will be true.

God has preordained everything before they were ever born, and that's a real foul thing to say over a person. And it's probably not even true because maybe that woman can learn to cook, or maybe she'll marry a chef, and she never needs to cook. You don't know, unless God tells you. And, why would He tell you? Why would He talk to you, if you're in your flesh? How do you expect to clearly hear

God if you're in your flesh? In your flesh is where the devil can easily *corrupt* communication.

Regarding this woman, you just don't know, do you? Best to ask Wisdom before you speak. Protect the reputation of your words, to not damage your credibility, so you can declare and decree in the spirit with authority.

It would be best to know what God says before you speak, than to have to try to walk it back. In this way you don't speak false things over people. You don't make yourself into a liar. And even if something evil or negative comes to pass, you don't make yourself into a *blind witch* by speaking or thinking something negative about that person who fell under evil. As a blind witch you don't realize that you do have authority in the spirit, but it is a negative authority for evil things. As a blind agent of evil, an agent of Satan you could be, without knowing it, cursing your enemy or your friend or a spouse or a child or an ex.

An ex? *Uh-huh.*

You know, all those *ever* and *never* proclamations, they are so bad. The relationship was great, but then the feelings turn, and the horrible things that people say over exes--, ex-boyfriends, ex-girlfriends, ex-wives, ex-husbands and ex-friends can be *too much.* When somebody's feeling rejected, or worse, condemned.

- *Oh, you know you're never gonna find another man like me.*
- *You're never gonna find another woman like me.* I heard a guy say once. "Well, isn't that the point?"
- *'No one's ever gonna want you."*

All those are word curses; don't do that. Don't say those words; just don't, especially since one or more of those exes, or all of them might also know how to pray and do return to sender prayers. You run the risk of getting back some of those words that you don't want for yourself. If you don't want those very same words spoken to you, don't say them, because they could be back on the way to you before you get them out of your mouth.

This makes the verse, A man shall have what he says a very real thing. And remember we all shall give account thereof in the day of judgment, (Matthew 12:36)

The blind witch may idly, ignorantly, foolishly, put stumbling blocks and barriers in a person's life, making it really hard for that person to proceed, or maybe even impossible for them to succeed.

I've seen young people and older people of age who are still at home with their parents. They are relegated to be there or they are soul tied to their parent or parents. Men can't leave and cleave. It's vampiric, as the old who have already lived most of their life now try to suck the life out of the young people in their world.

When *You're* Blind to It

Some of this book has been about people blindly cursing themselves. But there are some who are out there who are against you. It may or may not be blind to them but it's blind to you, because until you earnestly pray and ask God, you don't really know who's speaking *whatever* about you, or over you until their real intentions are made known to you. *Maybe you're the coworker that is being reported on to the coven at night by another coworker who is a blind witch.*

A witch likes to do things and appear blameless, so they can stay in their relationship with you, eyes on you, monitor you, see what you're doing. So, they come sometimes disguised as friends, and you will never suspect them except for God telling you. And they make believe that your friends, but they are really there to block what God has for you. They're really there to block what God has for you to do. They can even be your church buddies, and the day you decide to let your star shine, that's when they'll show themselves. These *monitoring spirits* are assigned to keep you limited, held back, locked down in life.

Gotta be careful of what you tell to whom. If you have problems, they're happy. But when you step up and start solving the problems of your life, stepping into God and what God has for you, they usually show who they really are.

They'll probably run away because they can't stand it. Go ahead, start fasting and praying and engaging in spiritual warfare, if they can't talk you out of it by some distraction or mind games, they're gonna run. The Fires of God will light up the unserious. You may then find out that you may not really have these *friends* anymore because they're gonna be gone. They can't stand the Fire.

And these are the, *It don't take all that* people. They want to keep you mediocre. They want to keep you from progressing. They'll play religion and socialize with you, *but* when you bring the Fire of God to the problems of your life, watch them change up on you.

Unfortunately, sometimes it could be the friend you love the most. It could be the friend since school or college. But you may find out at this time that this is a fake friend. Fake friends want to oppress you and lead you into mediocrity or keep you there. **Not so**, says the Lord. The Lord God created you for more than just average. He created you for success and abundance in Him.

In conclusion, don't spend so much time in a place of hurt over a lost fake friend. It was a fake friend. Be thankful that God has shown you this person and be thankful that not very much damage is done and move on in the Lord toward your destiny.

Prayer

61. Thank You, Lord, for Your presence. We ascribe glory and honor and greatness to Your Name, in the Name of Jesus.
62. Lord, let the Blood of Jesus that speaks better than the blood of Abel speak Mercy for me.
63. Lord, we have erred against Your commandments. Father, in the Name of Jesus, please forgive me in any area of my life where I've sinned against You. Please forgive me.
64. I plead the Blood of Jesus that it will speak to me from righteousness. Lord, have Mercy. Father, I ask for your Grace and Mercy. Lord, release me from every word curse that I have

spoken over another person, in anger and hatred and jealousy, rage, division, strife, and all works of the flesh; Lord cancel those blind witchcraft words and forgive me, in the Name of Jesus.

65. Father, please forgive every evil word curse that I've spoken over myself and over others, in the Name of Jesus. Render them null and void and forgive me for ever having spoken them, in the Name of Jesus.

66. Father, please restore any person that I have hurt in a blind rage, in the Name of Jesus.

67. Forgive me for evil words spoken over people with whom I've been in interpersonal relationships. Lord, I break all evil soul ties, I release them and wish them well and success in their lives, in the Name of Jesus.

68. Lord, where the person didn't realize what they were doing or what they were saying, like Jesus, I ask Father, forgive them for they did not know what they were doing.

69. Father do not let their words or those curses, hinder, block, steal, or kill me, in the Name of Jesus.

70. Those who are your enemies, Father, those who purposefully send evil in my direction to thwart my destiny, my purpose, my ministry, or the plan of God for my life, I return every word, every word curse, every arrow, every poison back to sender, in the Name of Jesus.

71. Father, I break every word curse ever spoken over me since my birth, in the Name of Jesus.

72. Lord, I bind every devil, who is opposing my finances and financial blessings, in the Name of Jesus.

73. Father, the blind witches who spoke those curses, may they repent as you deal with them and their sins, in the Name of Jesus.

74. Thank You for hearing and answering our prayers to You be all glory and honor, and praise, in the Name of Jesus, Amen.

Turned Over

(This chapter contains excerpts from my book, __Already Married In the Spirit__).

If you are under an evil dedication, it means your life and destiny have been turned over to the devil, with or without your knowledge. It could have been at birth, after you were born, when you were a young child, and you knew nothing about it. It could have been *before* you were born. It could have been *before* you were conceived; it could have been a *condition* of a conception ritual that one or both parents did to even get pregnant with you. That condition would be that the child now *belongs* to the idol (devil, demon) that helped them conceive.

It would be great to believe that you are righteous seed, but we don't know what folks have done to get the things they desired or felt that they needed--, even our own relatives.

If you have been "dedicated" that means that Satan has full control over your life.

Your parents could have innocently, ignorantly, or by tradition, tried to protect you by dedicating you to some *idol* that is known in their world to protect children and babies. People get dedicated to family or community idols. Those idols may include serpents, marine deities, idol *gods, or other evil spirits* that pose as good and helpful. Unless a person is a satanist or occultist, and at a certain level in a cult, the true identity of the "*gods'* they deal with is usually hidden.

75. Lord, release my life from every evil dedication by the power in the Blood of Jesus.
76. I release my life from every evil dedication, by the power in the Blood of Jesus.

Some types of evil dedication include the following:

- Coven dedication
- Sexual dedication
- Demonic dream dedication
- Evil marks dedication Let the blood flush out of me all inherited or self-acquired evil deposits in my system. Father Lord, as it is written that I should be strong in the Lord and in the power of His might, I ask that You be my might and strength all the days of my life.
- Curse dedication

How can you know if you've been dedicated?

Pray, ask the Lord and listen. The Holy Spirit will tell and or show you either in your waking life, or in a dream. Suspect evil dedication if any of these things are happening to you:

- Your life is crazy and seems out of control.
- Your dream life seems afflicted. For instance, you

may be summoned all over the place in your sleeping life.

- Your marital destiny is affected or afflicted.
- Nothing is working out where you live; territorial powers are ruling you.

You could be part of a collective captivity as evil dedications affect families, towns, neighborhoods, cities, even nations, and whole continents.

- You feel controlled or manipulated in life.
77. Every evil power controlling my life, release me and die, in the Name of Jesus.
78. Lord, release my life from every evil dedication, by the power in the Blood of Jesus.
79. I release my life from every evil dedication by the power in the Blood of Jesus.

Another sign of evil dedication is you are drawn to evil – well, you don't see evil as evil, you see demonic symbols, images, even satanic jewelry as something desirable to have. Somehow these things and images attract you, and you don't resist acquiring them. If you objectively look around your house and life you may find demonic symbols everywhere--, if you have been dedicated. And you don't see a thing in the world wrong with it.

I've seen a parade of spider tattoos, dragons, snakes, and other witchy and occultic things on a daily basis. No one forced these tattoos on the people; it's not like they were branded as slaves or property. But they desired to "brand" themselves, and they chose demonic images to place permanently on their own skin.

Ignorantly, a person could choose a totally satanic tattoo that they think is cool, and by having it on their skin, they draw a demon to him or herself. When you tattoo yourself, you mark yourself and when demons see the mark, you are identified as one of *theirs*. So then they come for you. They stay because they think they have married you. If you are already married in the spiritual realm, then how will you find or be able to marry your real spouse? Married in the spirit blocks you from getting married in the natural world. *Spirit spouse* and those other demons will fight you. They can put you in evil timelines so you miss divine connections, but if you happen to meet the right person that you are supposed to marry, the demons will fight you and they will fight the person who is interested in you, as well.

Your name may be a reflection of your having been dedicated, or your dedication chose your name. Your name, if it is an evil name, can also draw evil *spirits*. What names are you calling in your house? Does your child, or even your pet have an evil name? Find out and change it because **every time you call that name you are summoning the demon associated with that name.**

Ritualistic bathing in rivers, the ocean, and other waters.

- Sitting under a marine kingdom pastor or priest knowingly or unknowingly.

Certain festivals, such as marine festivals, or serpent dedication festivals can initiate or dedicate a person of any age. Some you don't even have to guess about, such as the Festival of the Steel Phallus in Japan; people take their children to these festivals. And there are other festivals that initiate and renew evil dedication.

Sleeping on white cloth given to you by fetish priests, sorcerers, witch doctors, and demonic "pastors." The wearing of certain garments, especially being a part of a white garment church. Any ritual can initiate a person.

Don't stop praying, and declaring:

80. I release my life from every evil initiation by the power in the Blood of Jesus.

81. I release my life from every evil dedication by the power in the Blood of Jesus.
82. I am married to Jesus, Satan leave me alone, in the Name of Jesus.
83. I bear in my body the marks of the Lord Jesus Christ, by the power in the Blood of Jesus, I declare Jesus is my husband, and I am not or any longer married to any devil, demon, idol, false *god*, or Satan, in the Name of Jesus.
84. I snatch my child back from the clutches of the devil because of evil initiations that I was not aware of, or dedications made in ignorance or accidentally, in the Name of Jesus. I declare my child will serve the only Living God, and never Satan, in the Name of Jesus.

Everyday Witchy Stuff

Manipulation can be so simple or so complicated. The manipulator can manipulate messages and phone calls. They can fake a letter or an email. A Nigerian prince comes to mind. Manipulators can manipulate other manipulators as well, the last report I saw was that the latest Nigerian prince was an old white guy from Louisiana. The only thing that surprised me there was that he was not from Florida.

Manipulation comes off as a little more subtle than control, domination, or intimidation because it is more occultic. The control is hidden and many times, at least in soap operas it may take up to a year for the victim of manipulation to figure out what even happened to him or her. In real life it could take years or even a lifetime to figure out if your life has been controlled by witches or other evil devil agents.

Control, domination and intimidation is also witchcraft, but it is in your face witchcraft. It is usually the act of the warlock type person with threats, threats of loss, and threats of harm if the person doesn't do what they want them to do. They may say things like:

- *You'd better check yourself before you wreck yourself.*
- *If you don't lose weight, I'm going to put you out and get a new girlfriend, or a new wife.*
- Domination, "I am the man, and you do what I say."
- Intimidation- If you don't do what I say, you don't know what I will do to you."
- I brought you into this world, and I will take you out.
- Blackmail of any kind is for control and manipulation; it is

witchcraft. Emotional blackmail is done with words. If the person doesn't realize that they are doing it is blind witchcraft.

Let's include trickery and deception in this. TV Sitcoms are riddled with this. The TV show, *I Love Lucy*, and just about every other one that we've seen since then are full of schemes and plots and plans to get something or to get Ricky (her husband) to do something. Pretty much the same plots are in modern shows, except now the witches are out there in the open. Occultic themes, magic, magic, magic—, all that is witchcraft.

Getting what you want by any means is witchcraft. The person who wants what they want and will be willing to get it by any means usually steps into witchcraft either immediately or eventually.

Jesus was tempted in the Wilderness to turn stones into bread. How badly did He want some bread, after all, He had been fasting 40 days and 40 nights? In that time frame God had destroyed the entire world with Noah's Flood. If Jesus had turned that stone into bread He would have stepped over into witchcraft because this would have been AGAINST the *Will* of God.

Jesus is neither a witch, nor a warlock, so neither should any of us be.

Rebellion is as the sin of witchcraft. Opposing God, opposing the will of God is witchcraft. Witchcraft is an evil imagination and the willingness to carry it out--, no matter what.

My God shall supply all my needs according to His riches in Glory, by Christ Jesus. Amen.

- Domestic abuse is witchcraft – it is domination and intimidation to control.
- Financial abuse is witchcraft, it is for control.
- Racism is witchcraft—it is for domination and to control.
- Colorism is witchcraft.
- Sexism and misogyny is witchcraft for domination and control.

- Elder abuse is domination and witchcraft.
- Playing mind games with people is witchcraft.

Do you need more examples? There are so many more ways that people are blind witches. If you are not dealing with people honestly, then you are fully in or bordering near witchcraft. We all need to do better.

Magic Versus Miracles

Alchemy is the practice of trying to turn something into something else. The first books on alchemy were written by Moses of Alexandria (Greece), aka, Moses the Alchemist is NOT the Moses of the Old Testament Bible.

Man, in his own power, or with or by the powers that he is invoking and employing, whether he knows it or not are ever trying to turn something into something else. That something else is usually something desired or perceived to be of greater value.

We see alchemy in magic, movies, fairytales. It stems from ancient practices . Wonder where they got that idea? Oh, in the Wilderness Temptations, the devil may have said something like, *Jesus, if you are hungry why don't you turn these stones into bread?*

In the Old Testament the Hebrews were to make bricks without straw, and how is that even possible?

Well, in the fairytale, Rumpelstiltskin, the miller's daughter was to turn straw into gold. The miller was already operating a mill and turning wheat into flour, so why not ask this girl to turn straw into gold?

Turning things into gold requires magic and magic is witchcraft. Greedy or needy man, why don't you turn this mundane metal into gold? That is alchemy.

We are taught to use our imaginations as children and many parents think that is great. But in pushing our children to the unbelievable, the unforeseeable and by doing so we may be teaching them to invoke spiritual help from *powers* and *spirits* that we may not know where they are coming from.

They come from the underworld, the dark kingdom. God doesn't have angels that do ungodly things. This is why

Scripture says we are to cast down imaginations and every high thing that exalts itself against the knowledge of God.

The intent? The lust for a thing, the desire to have it at all costs usually doesn't involve much cost to the person who wants it—the cost is usually at the expense of someone else.

So, what's the difference between magic and miracles?

Big difference.

Magic employs demonic *spirits*—always. That is how magic works. **Magic is the attempt to influence persons and events** by invoking superhuman powers: it is "the science of the occult." Whenever magic is present a soul or souls are being snatched.

Miracles are simply acts of God, creating an astonishing or amazing event that can only be explained by the presence of the Most High God. The blessings of the Lord make one rich and He adds no sorry with it. Amen.

She's No Lady & This is Not Justice

The lady on the cover of this book was chosen purposefully. She's really not a lady and she does not represent real justice. Oxford defines witchcraft as the use of magic to help or harm people. Witchcraft always harms someone because the person using it is harmed, ultimately. To interface with demons and devils and evil *spirits*, the operator has sold their soul and become an evil human agent for the devil.

The person the evil agent is using it **for** will be harmed, in the long run. Let's say the agent has created a love potion. This potion may render short term results that the sender and user like, but in the long run, not so much. The victim of the love potion may think he's happy, but is he? He is being made to do things against his own will. The person that the victim is supposed to be married to is harmed, and the children that they were supposed to produce in their marriage are not; that is harm to the plan of God.

Lady Justice, edited was chosen because those who practice witchcraft believe themselves judge, jury and executioner. They are doling out their own version of justice, which is just what they want. It is based on the flesh and works of the flesh, whether it is revenge or the lust for money for doing these magical things for people.

Divorce Them

85. Let there be a divorce now, on the gates of my eyes, on the gates of my body, soul, and spirit, in the Name of Jesus.
86. I divorce him now. I divorce the strongman, in the Name of Jesus.
87. I am divorcing Satan, the strongman of my family bloodline, in the Name of Jesus.
88. Any network that I have ever gotten myself into, any alliances, evil covenants, groups that I ever got involved in, I get out now, by the power in the Blood of Jesus.
89. I break every evil covenant, and I dismantle every curse that has come over my life and my family, in Jesus' Name.
90. As the parent I take my authority to command a divorce from the

strongman on behalf of my children, in Jesus' Name.

91. I break every soul tie with every spiritual entity that has come into my life by any means, in the Name of Jesus.

92. I come boldly to the Throne of Grace, and I ask the Father to grant me divorce from all of these evil entities, in Jesus' Name.

93. I divorce Satan, by the power in the Blood of Jesus.

94. I ask the Blood of Jesus to nullify and destroy any evil initiation that was forced on me, on my life, in the Name of Jesus.

95. I divorce it now, in the Name of Jesus.

96. Blood of Jesus dismiss the initiation that was conducted on me, in Jesus' Name.

97. You *spirit*, you man, you woman, whoever you may be, today in the Name of Jesus, I divorce you, I divorce you, I divorce you, in the Name of Jesus.

98. Lord, enter a decree of permanent divorce from these demons, in the Name of Jesus.
99. I divorce every evil human, astral projecting agent, I condemn you. I divorce you, whether I knew you married me or not, in Jesus' Name.
100. Blood of Jesus speak for me, dismiss, break every evil initiation, in the Name of Jesus.
101. Wrong sex, I renounce you, I denounce, I condemn you, and every iniquity and evil contract you have allowed in my life, in the Name of Jesus.
102. Illegal sex, I renounce you, I denounce you and every iniquity and evil contract you have allowed in my life, in the Name of Jesus
103. Uncovenanted sex., I renounce you, I denounce you and every iniquity and evil contract you have allowed in my life, in the Name of Jesus.
104. Unapproved sex, unsanctioned sex, nonconsensual sex, I renounce you, I denounce you and every

iniquity and evil contract you have allowed in my life, in the Name of Jesus.

105. In dreams, parties, in schools, at work, in hotels, at church... no matter where wrong sex happened, I break your evil effects over my life, in the Name of Jesus.

106. *Spirit spouse* and all of your effects get out of my mind, get out of my body, get out of the path of my destiny, in Jesus' Name.

107. I divorce every evil *spirit* passed on to me to open the gates of hell against me, in the Name of Jesus.

108. I divorce Satan and all your servants and all your serpents, in the Name of Jesus.

109. I break all your covenants and contracts against me, in the Name of Jesus.

110. I am married to Jesus. Jesus, as my legal husband, declare me single from every devil, demon, *familiar spirit,* strongman, principality, ruler, Satan, himself, every evil human agent, in the Name of Jesus. (X5). Amen.

Jezebel

Jezebel was about the worst witch in the Bible. Jezebel is a *spirit* that can inhabit the souls of either men or women. If there is a Jezebel *spirit*, there is an Ahab *spirit* nearby. Sometimes both *spirits* are in the same person. Ever notice a person with a split personality? *Uh huh.*

Jezebel hated the prophets of God and killed them. She fed the prophets who did her bidding at her own table. No doubt, it was food dedicated to idols; therefore, she initiated them, whether they knew it or not.

She was a queen, with authority over an entire kingdom. Around her, Ahab was very passive, which is a hallmark of the Ahab *spirit*, so Jezebel was able to turn that kingdom the way she wanted. She turned the worship of the kingdom from God to Ba'al. This amounts to taking the whole kingdom to Hell. She framed and had Naboth killed to steal his vineyard.

It did not turn out well for her, as is the case of all witches, believe it or not. The spirit of Jehu is still operating in the Earth also; he is the one who did away with Jezebel.

In today's terms a jezebel is a wanton, sleazy woman, which implies that this *spirit* will use everything she has to seduce, manipulate, control, dominate and intimidate. Jezebel is the name of a very strong witchcraft *spirit*. Men also can use their masculine wiles to seduce, as this *spirit* is not only found in women.

Renounce & Repent

Why do I have to renounce and repent? I didn't do anything. If you're asking that you're not ready to let go of this *spirit*. If you are asking that you are not ready to renounce the initiation or participation in the dark halls of witchcraft.

They say that folks don't tell or expose what they are still using, but when they are ready to let go of it, they will gladly let it be known to whomever may be listening. We overcome by the Blood of the Lamb and the word of our testimony. As well our repentance is pivotal to our relationship in Christ. We pray that God is listening because that's who we want to repent to.

Get It Out of There

111.   Cleanse me, Lord. Cleanse me
from all evil initiations and from all
things occultic, satanic, and witchcraft
related. Show me things that I am
blind to. Remove every evil mark off
of me and every evil marker out of my
blood. Cleanse me, cleanse my
system, cleanse my foundation,
cleanse my bloodline, in the Name of
Jesus.

You just happen to like this and proclaim
that it is *style*. Well, it looks witchy. Does
God like it? Then get it out of there.

112.   Long nails, witchy nails, pointy
nails, long nails, curled nails, anything
that is or looks like demonic
ornamentations on the nails, hair, or

body, Lord, make me hate it, in the Name of Jesus.

Tattoos of any kind, but spiders, skulls, dragons, pentagrams and other satanic, demonic and witchy marks and images. It's the style? *Whose style?* The world's style. So, does God like it?

No. This repulses God, while it attracts witches and other entities of the dark kingdom; they will be attracted to those marks on a person's body, or in a person's house. It is said that demons who recognize your marks as they are flying over will stop when they see "their" mark. Then it is said that they stop to begin to feast on your life because they are eaters of flesh and drinkers of blood, and you have identified yourself as one of *theirs*, or one that has been marked as available for them to feast on.

The most dangerous of things is having the names of dead people inscribed on your body. That is another calling card for demons. Of even more importance is the names of living people on your body because when you die, you will take those names down to the grave with you. Have you thought about this, at all? While these are your "loved ones", are you some ancient king and you take people with you to the grave? Do not take your living loved ones to the grave with you when you go by having their names inscribed on you.

These are common things that witches wear, use, or are attracted to. If it is not of God, get it out of there, get it off of you.

False Pastors, False Prophets & False Prayers

Careful of who you let pray for you and over you, especially if it involves the laying on of hands.

Everyone who claims to be of God may not be. I've run into a few in my life. I'm not speaking of saved folks who are trying to live sin free, but they fall, repent and get back up. I'm talking about true sinners, satanists, witches, warlocks and such who are pretending to be saved. Why? For fame. For power. For money. They go into churches as leaders and look for sacrifices, because they need sacrifices. Sacrifices are how any altar works, especially evil altars.

If a pastor can take an entire church to hell, don't you think the devil will notice his influence and give him position and perks and power and money in this life?

You'd better know.

The point is that those false pastors, false prophets, and false prayers could be initiating you and everyone else into the kingdom of darkness but have you thinking its God. This includes initiation into witchcraft.

Just because something is spiritual doesn't make it God.

Folks, if you are seeking deliverance for example, you know something is wrong in your life but you're not sure what it is, so you go to a place or a person for help, but they never tell you that anything is wrong with you, that's a problem. They either are spiritually blind themselves or they want you to stay jacked up. As long as you are incorrect spiritually, you are a target for the devil. The only thing that is missing is an evil human agent. At that "church" or wherever you went for help, you could be looking right at that person, right at that evil human agent.

We hear reports of pretenders all the time, they are false pastors, false prophets; do not heed what they are saying. Do not sit under that. Do not let them lay hands on you. You must know the Word of God for yourself.

Some are people that claim to be praying for others are not. Some who claim to be helping them, and are actually changing them, are trapping them, initiating them into the dark kingdom, or setting them up for sacrifice. Folks, if you feel led, let others pray for you or with you, but that doesn't mean that you don't pray yourself, for yourself.

113. I renounce and condemn witchcraft in every form, by any name, no matter where it came from or how long it has been with me, in the Name of Jesus.

114. Lord, by Your own Blood, purge and transfuse my blood ridding it of every evil mark of witchcraft, in the Name of Jesus.

115. Lord, I jump the bloodline of my family, and escape all evil, witchcraft, and occultism in my ancestry, in the Name of Jesus.

116. Lord, purge and heal my foundation, in Jesus' Name.

117. Every form of evil initiation and every evil word that has been spoken over my life, I break it now, in Jesus' Name.

118. Anyone that has tried to make me an agent with or without my knowledge, I renounce this, I condemn it, in the Name of Jesus.

119. I come out from every evil association, every evil group, every evil meeting, in the Name of Jesus.

120. Today I publicly renounce, and reject and refuse to be a part of such gathering, such meetings, forever, in the Name of Jesus.

121. Every evil prayer that has been prayed over me, every evil word that

have been spoken over me, I renounce it today, in the Name of Jesus.

122.   Every evil hand that has been laid on me, draw back and wither, in the Name of Jesus.

123.   Father, reverse the effects of every evil touch and laying on of hands over me and my family, in Jesus' Name.

124.   I belong to Jesus Christ. I am a child of God; I am in Christ, I am in Christ. Amen.

125.   Father, I reject being a part of any form of witchcraft, being an evil agent, or being in any evil group, in the Name of Jesus.

126.   Every evil word spoken over my life, I reject it, in the Name of Jesus.

127.   Lord, if I'm a blind witch deliver me today, in Jesus' Name.(X3)

128.   Lord, restore my soul, in the Name of Jesus. (X5)

129.   Lord, with Mercy toward me, deal with the pretenders by your Righteous Judgement so they don't take others to hell, in the Name of Jesus.

130. Lord, stop the hand of anyone who has planned or is planning to kill me, in the Name of Jesus.

131. Satan, I'm not your candidate for sacrifice, I am in Christ, in Jesus' Name.

132. Lord, cover every gift, seed, or offering, or anything of value that I have put on any evil altar with the Blood of Jesus.

133. I do not worship Satan. I do not worship devils, I do not worship demons, idol *gods, goddesses*, or rulers of darkness or evil principalities, and I do not bring them offerings, in the Name of Jesus.

134. If I have ignorantly given an offering to the dark kingdom in any form, at any time and in any place, I call it back right now, in Jesus 'Name.

135. Lord, have Your Mighty Angels recover every misplaced offering put on any cvil altar at any time, in the Name of Jesus. Silence that worship, in Jesus' Name.

136. Everything stolen from me in this process be returned to me,

immediately, seven-fold, in the Name of Jesus.

137. Lord, by the Power of the Holy Ghost make me FREE and free indeed, in the Name of Jesus.

138. Lord, if I'm a blind witch, deliver me today, in the Name of Jesus.

139. Lord, burn my file in the spirit that is in possession by any evil entity in the Name of Jesus.

140. Lord, let them forget my name and lose my location, forever, in the Name of Jesus.

141. Take my name off every evil register, in the Name of Jesus.

142. Satan, I declare I'm not your candidate and I am not your agent; I do not work for you, in the Name of Jesus – I am in Christ.

143. Lord, arise and contend with all those who do not get the memo or who pretend not to understand that I am OUT of the dark kingdom, I am not a part of it and I am not available to it in any way, in Jesus' Name.

In The Dream

You have been initiated into witchcraft when you see any of this in the dream:

- Dream pollution
- Dream defilement
- Evil exchange
- Eating in the dream .
- Sex in the dream.
- Hair cut in the dream.
- Nails being cut in the dream.
- Marks cut on the body.
- Swimming in the river,
- Notice strange marks on the body.

You should have canceled any and all of those initiation dreams immediately when you woke up, but if you did not, be sure to pray all the prayers in this book and be set free.

144. I cancel every evil initiation dream, in the Name of Jesus.
145. I cancel every dream pollution, every defilement, every evil exchange that has made me to enter into any evil covenant in the dream, without even realizing it, in the Name of Jesus.
146. Lord, break that yoke of evil initiation and evil covenant, in the Name of Jesus.

Proceed to seven days fasting and prayers. If you can't fast the full seven days, fast some hours or some meals of the day. If you cannot do that, medically, then fast your favorite food for 30 days. Be sure to dedicate your fast to the Lord.

Is not this the fast that I have chosen? to loose the bands of wickedness, to undo the heavy burdens, and to let the oppressed go free, and that ye break every yoke? (Isaiah 58:6)

Your covenant with death will be annulled, And your agreement with Sheol will not stand; When the overflowing scourge passes through, Then you will be trampled down by it. (Isaiah 28:18)

As you make these prayers, decrees, and declarations you will see a change in your life. Your dreams will be better--, more divine. You will feel more peaceful. You will feel the presence of Wisdom with you when you speak. Doors of opportunity that were shut will be opening for you. People will change; many will show you favor. But others may be absent, if they did not have good intentions toward you all along.

You may lose interest in being around some people you used to hang out with. Your prayer partners may change, and thank God for that. Because of these renunciations those who were on assignment and had an agenda concerning you will realize that they are defeated, and they will either go away, or God will take them away from your life.

Stay prayerful. Pray for yourself, pray for those you have authority over, such as your own children. Intercede for those who the Lord puts on your heart or those who cannot pray for themselves in this season.

147. Every evil food initiating me into demonic covenants, catch Fire, in the Name of Jesus.

148. Let the Blood of Jesus and the Fire of God cancel every evil initiation against me or my destiny, in Jesus' Name.

149. Any of my glory that has been stolen from me through evil initiation and evil covenants, come back to me, in the Name of Jesus.

150. Every evil association delaying my progress, scatter, by Fire, in Jesus' Name.

151. Any power that is using initiation dreams to kill my star, die by Fire, in the Name of Jesus.

152. Every power attacking my star, run mad and die, in the Name of Jesus.

153. Every witchcraft dedication to keep me caged or in bondage, be destroyed by Fire.

154. Every initiation carried out against me in the dream or waking life, I cancel you by the power in the Blood of Jesus.

155. Every agent of witchcraft attached to me, to frustrate my life, die by Fire, in the Name of Jesus.

156. Let the Fire of God cancel and destroy the effects of every evil initiation upon my life, ministry, marriage, family, destiny

157. Anything that has been taken from my destiny by the wicked to bewitch me, Lord, scatter it, in Jesus' Name.

158. By the Blood of Jesus, I nullify every evil dream bringing spiritual problems into my life, in the Name of Jesus.

159. Lord, nullify the effects of every evil dream, in the Name of Jesus.

160. I seal these declarations across every dimension, realm and timeline, past present and future with the Blood of Jesus and the Spirit of Promise.

161. Every retaliation because of this book, these words, these prayers, these decrees and declarations against the author, the reader, and anyone praying these prayers, backfire against the sender 1,000,000 times and without Mercy, in the Name of Jesus. **AMEN**.

Dear Reader

Thank you for acquiring and reading this book. I pray that it has spoken to you to make you look at yourself thoroughly. I pray you will make any necessary changes so that you and your life glorify the Lord.

As we work out our own salvation with fear and trembling, we make sure that we are not embroiled, entrapped, or initiated into any kind of witchcraft.

Be strong in the Lord, and be blessed, in the Name of Jesus, Amen.

Dr. Marlene Miles

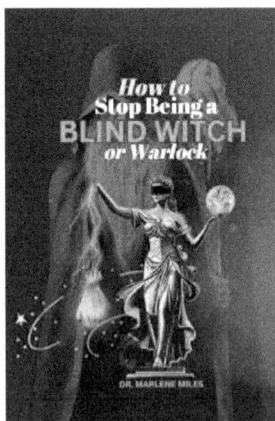

Prayer books by this author

While most books by this author have prayer points either throughout the book or at the end, there are some books that are only prayers. You just open up the book and pray. They are listed below:

Prayers Against Barrenness: *For Success in Business and Life*

Fruit of the Womb: *Prayers Against Barrenness*

Beauty Curses, *Warfare Prayers Against*
https://a.co/d/5Xlc20M

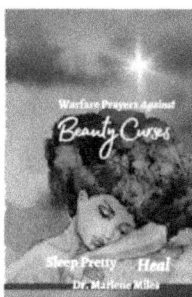

Courts of Marriage: Prayers for Marriage in the Courts of Heaven
(prayerbook) https://a.co/d/cNAdgAq

Courtroom Warfare @ Midnight
(prayerbook) https://a.co/d/5fc7Qdp

Demonic Cobwebs *(prayerbook)*
https://a.co/d/fp9Oa2H

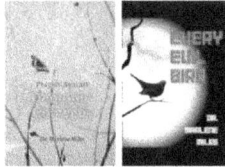

Every Evil Bird https://a.co/d/hF1kh1O

Gates of Thanksgiving

Spirits of Death, Hell & the Grave, Pass Over Me and My House

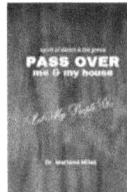

Throne of Grace: Courtroom Prayer

Warfare Prayer Against Poverty
https://a.co/d/bZ61lYu

Other books by this author

AK: The Adventures of the Agape Kid

AMONG SOME THIEVES

Ancestral Powers

Anti-Marriage, *The Spirit of*

Backstabbers https://a.co/d/gi8iBxf

Barrenness, *Prayers Against*
https://a.co/d/feUltIs

Battlefield of Marriage, *The*

Beware of the Dog: Prayers Against
Dogs in the Dream
https://a.co/d/6TGpKOf

Blindsided: *Has the Old Man
Bewitched You?* https://a.co/d/5O2fLLR

Break Free from Collective Captivity

Caged Life: *Get Out Alive!*
https://a.co/d/9ibl8W3

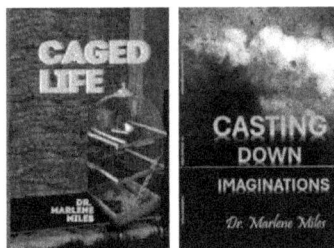

Casting Down Imaginations
https://a.co/d/d51Ehcz

Churchzilla, The Wanna-Be, Supposed-to-be Bride of Christ

Curses of Blind Men

Demonic Cobwebs (prayerbook)

Demonic Time Bombs

Demons & Destruction at Noonday

Demons Hate Questions

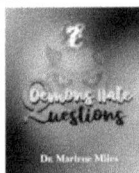

https://a.co/d/61FWoiY

Devil Loves Trauma, *The*

Devil Weapons: Unforgiveness, Bitterness,…

The Devourers: Thieves of Darkness 2

Do Not Swear by the Moon

Don't Refuse Me, Lord (4 book series)

https://a.co/d/idP34LG

Dream Defilement
https://a.co/d/2b1TeCv

The Emptiers: *Thieves of Darkness, 1*
https://a.co/d/5I4n5mc

Evil Touch

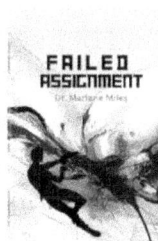

Failed Assignment

Fantasy Spirit Spouse
https://a.co/d/hW7oYbX

FAT Demons (The): *Breaking Demonic Curses*

The Fold (5-book series)

- The Fold (Book 1)
- Name Your Seed (Book 2)
- The Poor Attitudes of Money (3)
- Do Not Orphan Your Seed (4)
- For the Sake of the Gospel (5)
- My Sowing Journal

Gang Ups: Touch Not God's Anointed

Getting Rid of Evil Spiritual Food
https://a.co/d/f9OG1qH

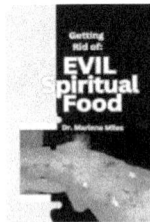

got HEALING? Verses for Life

got LOVE? Verses for Life

Motherboard (The) - *Soul Prosperity Series*

Name Your Seed

Occupy: *Until I Return*

Plantation Souls

Players Gonna Play

Power Money: Nine Times the Tithe

https://a.co/d/gRt41gy

The Power of Wealth *(forthcoming)*

Powers Above

The Robe, Part 1, The Lessons of Joseph

The Robe, Part II, The Lessons of Joseph

Seasons of Grief

Seasons of Waiting

Seasons of War

Second Marriage, Third--, *Any Marriage*

https://a.co/d/6m6GN4N

Sift You Like Wheat

Six Men Short: What Has Happened to all the Men?

Sleep Afflictions & Really Bad Dreams

Soul Prosperity soul prosperity series 3

https://a.co/d/5p8YvCN

Souls Captivity soul prosperity series 2

The Spirit of Poverty

StarStruck

SUNBLOCK

The Swallowers: *Thieves of Darkness,* 3

Take It Back

This Is NOT That: How to Keep
Demons from Coming at You

Time Is of the Essence

Too Many Wives: *Why You Have Lady
Problems*

Tormenting Spirits
https://a.co/d/dAogEJf

Toxic Souls

Triangular Power *(series)*

- Powers Above
- SUNBLOCK
- Do Not Swear by the Moon
- STARSTRUCK

Uncontested Doom

Unguarded Hours, *The*

Unseen Life, *The* (forthcoming)

Upgrade: How to Get Out of Survival Mode

- Toxic Souls (Book 2 of series)
- Legacy (Book 3 of series)

The Wasters: *Thieves of Darkness*, Bk 2
https://a.co/d/bUvI9Jo

What Have You to Declare? What Do You Have With You from Where You've Been?

When I Was A Child, *I Prayed As a Child*

When the Devourer is Rebuked

https://a.co/d/1HVv8oq

When You See Blood
https://a.co/d/edmlUKH

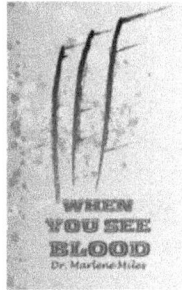

The Wilderness Romance *A series* about conducting a Godly relationship and marriage with someone who is a Wilderness person. It is about how to recognize it and navigate through it. These books are about how not to get caught up in such.

- *The Social Wilderness*
- *The Sexual Wilderness*
- *The Spiritual Wilderness*

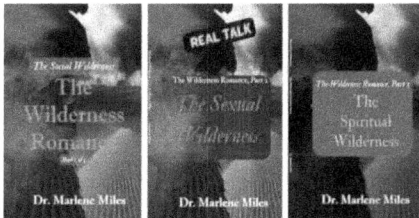

Other Series

The Fold (a series on Godly finances)
https://a.co/d/4hz3unj

Soul Prosperity Series https://a.co/d/bz2M42q

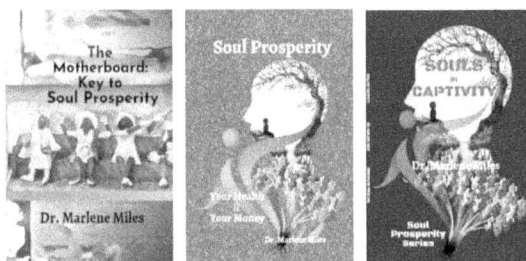

Spirit Spouse books

https://a.co/d/9VehDSo

https://a.co/d/97sKOwm

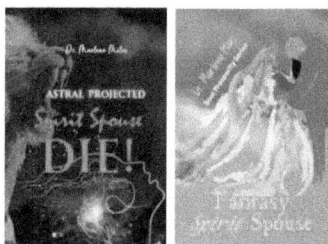

Thieves of Darkness series

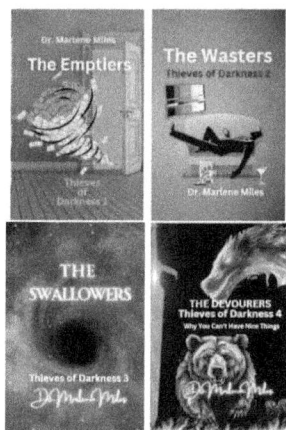

Triangular Powers https://a.co/d/aUCjAWC

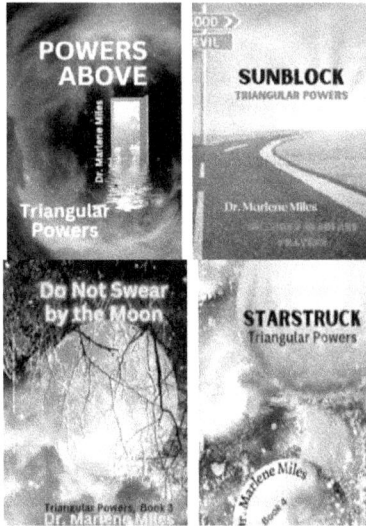

Upgrade (series) *How to Get Out of Survival Mode* https://a.co/d/aTERhXO

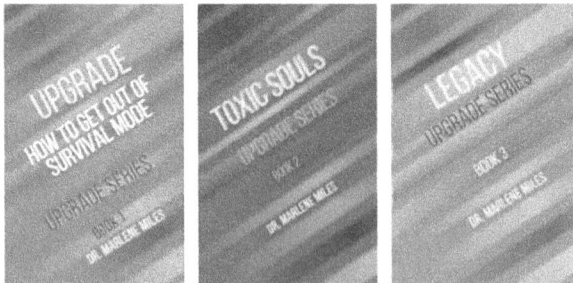

www.ingramcontent.com/pod-product-compliance
Lightning Source LLC
LaVergne TN
LVHW021347080426
835508LV00020B/2156